The Believer's Blueprint

Gabriel Gauthier

Saint Petersburg, Florida

Copyright © 2020 Gabriel Gauthier

Print ISBN: 978-1-64718-833-7
Epub ISBN: 978-1-64718-834-4
Mobi ISBN: 978-1-64718-835-1

Published by BookLocker.com, Inc., St. Petersburg, Florida.

Printed on acid-free paper.

BookLocker.com, Inc.
2020

First Edition

Table of Contents

Dedication

I would like to dedicate this devotional to my wife and my children. Amanda, you have been my rock and such an encourager when I lacked the courage in myself. To my girls which serve as an inspiration for my sermons every week and teach me every day how to see the world through a child's eyes.

To my dad and mom who are my greatest role models. Who still serve tirelessly and have always loved us unconditionally. To my brother and sister who have always been there for me and supported all my crazy ideas. To the rest of my family and friends who have always prayed for me and believed in me. To Prince of Peace, the incredible church that I have the honor of pastoring.

This one is for the builder, the dreamer and those that refuse to give up on their dreams. Keep going. You're closer than you think.

Introduction

I know you have read many books, manuals, and devotionals before, but this one might be outside of the realm of what you would consider a "devotional." This small book is something that God gave to me in a dream and gave me specific instructions about. The first thing that He spoke to me was how He wanted to build the body of Christ up, but wanted them to know that just like His son Jesus was a builder on the earth, He is still into building today. Jesus carried His Father's characteristics. Just like Jesus was a carpenter and creator, God is trying to give us the same design in having us build up our lives, our families, our jobs, our finances, and everything that is connected to us. If you look in the book of Ephesians, you see that God gives the fivefold ministry to the church for the building up of the saints (Ephesians 4:11).

Our lives are built around a blueprint designed by God.

11 For I know the plans I have for you," declares the Lord, "plans to prosper you and not to harm you, plans to give you hope and a future. Jeremiah 29:11 (NIV)

This word was given to Jeremiah, right before his people went into Babylonian captivity for 70 years. This is not just that God knew the plans that He had for Jeremiah, but He was speaking to His people through Jeremiah.

1

And the same way that God knew the plans that He had for Jeremiah, God knows the plans that He has for you.

This book speaks to the construct of a design and the different elements that go into building. The Believer's Blueprint was developed and designed in my heart for you. Through this book and with God's help, every day you are going to be building up a different part of your life. Some days symbolize a part of a house, others are different areas that we need God to help us in.

Additionally, there will be daily declarations that are included. Our words have power. The book of Hebrews registers that "the worlds were framed by the word of God" (Hebrews 11:3). God used words to create and since we are made in His likeness and image, we also have the power to create with our words. These daily declarations will help to create the world that you desire to live in. When we build it God's way and use His word to do it, we begin to see what He has purposed for us to see and live in the fullness of His promises.

Rome wasn't built in a day. We live and build our lives in phases. Today, you might want to build on your self-esteem and your personal growth. Next month, you want to read this entire blueprint again and build your family back up. Either way you choose to do it, do it knowing that God is going to give you the grace to do whatever you put your mind and will to do. So let's get started.

Day 1 – Consider

Today's Scripture: Luke 14:28-30 (NIV)

[28] *"Suppose one of you wants to build a tower. Won't you first sit down and estimate the cost to see if you have enough money to complete it?* [29] *For if you lay the foundation and are not able to finish it, everyone who sees it will ridicule you,* [30] *saying, 'This person began to build and wasn't able to finish.'*

Today's Thought:

One of the lessons I've learned in life is that we start things off with great zeal, strength, energy and enthusiasm. Halfway through the project or through whatever we chose to do, we lost the enthusiasm because it either took longer than we expected, cost more than we projected, or other things popped up along the way.

One of the things that the Bible calls us to do is to sit back before we start anything, and actually consider the cost and the time that a project is going to take. This means that we should consider the sacrifice that something we desire to do is going to actually take. As an example, think about a person that was watching the cooking channel one day and saw a chef make an incredible homemade apple pie. After seeing how easy it looked, they went to the supermarket and bought all the things the recipe required. When they got home and into the kitchen, they read through the recipe that once looked simple to make, and now are having trouble making the apple pie-making process look as easy as it looked on television. Halfway through the baking process, they throw all the ingredients down at the failed attempt to make an apple pie, and go down to the local bakery and just buy an apple pie to cure their appetite for it. This example shows us the reality that as human beings, we get very enthusiastic and lose that same enthusiasm very quickly because things didn't go as quickly as we thought they would.

If you look at your life today, you can probably see where you didn't finish something that you started. Even this devotional is something that you have to consider before you fully submerge yourself into it. In order for this entire devotional to make sense, you have to read the entire thing from beginning to end. God will give you the strength to do start and to finish it, but you have to commit to it. If you are going to do this, do it! If you're going to go back to school, do it! If you are going to embark upon a new career, do it! Do it with all your strength and ask God to give you the endurance to complete it.

Today's Declaration:

Lord, today I need your help. I am embarking on a journey to find the blueprint to my life. I need your strength and your direction to help me finish the race I've started. Today, I declare wisdom, direction and focus to lead my life. I will not be distracted by how long it might take or the things that might come along the way. I have considered the sacrifice required for this, and today I stand on the truth that I will run and finish what you've called for me to do.

In Jesus name, Amen!

Day 2 – The Will to Work

Today's Scripture: Philippians 2:12-13 (NIV)

[12] Therefore, my dear friends, as you have always obeyed—not only in my presence, but now much more in my absence—continue to work out your salvation with fear and trembling, [13] for it is God who works in you to will and to act in order to fulfill his good purpose.

Today's Thought:

For some, the first day is always the easiest. Just like when you're at a new job on the first day, they might let you go earlier than usual, or they might take it easy on you and not work you too hard. Reality sets in when job duties have been given, expectations have been set, and your job is really on the line. This usually happens within a month or so, but it feels like the second day on the job and you're already moving mountains.

The text today reminds us about the will to do things. We have to learn to ask God for the will to work to fulfill His purpose for our lives. You can have the greatest plans in mind and say to yourself that you're going back to school, but unless you actually register for the classes, that goal is going to stay a goal. I recently went back to school to pursue a degree, but no one filled out the application for me. I had to do it myself and then follow through when classes began. Your will becomes the vehicle by which your purpose is taken to fulfillment. I've seen that this is the place where God's grace works the best. Because when we cannot find it within ourselves to fulfill His will and can't seem to get the motor running, His grace, if asked for, will give you the will to do what you wouldn't have done on your own.

Now, I do say this with a disclosure: God will do what you're unable to do. God will not do what you're unwilling to do. This is a heavy responsibility because now I have to look at my heart and keep my priorities in order. Some people want to do God's will because they feel that's the only way they are going to get known. Some people are doing God's will to make Jesus known. Which are you? What are your motives? This is such a huge prerequisite to building.

Ask yourself, "Why am I building this? What are the reasons I'm building this?" You can apply this to any part of your life, not just ministry. I guarantee if you ask yourself this before making any important decision and committing, you will either start it and finish it, or you will reconsider and go back to the drawing board. This will save you time and save you plenty of money.

Today's Declaration:

Lord, today I pray for the grace to will my way through what I am currently embarking upon. If you don't give me the will to do it, it cannot be done. Today, I place all pride and selfishness to the side and focus on the goal, which is your purpose for my life. I ask because you said it was for your good purpose and pleasure. Although I might not have all the details right now, I thank you because in due time, it will all make sense and have great reason and purpose for me, my family and all that surround me.

In Jesus name, Amen!

Day 3 – The Right Workers

Today's Scripture: Matthew 18:18-19 (NLT)

[18] *"I tell you the truth, whatever you forbid on earth will be forbidden in heaven, and whatever you permit on earth will be permitted in heaven.*

[19] *"I also tell you this: If two of you agree here on earth concerning anything you ask, my Father in heaven will do it for you.* [20] *For where two or three gather together as my followers, I am there among them."*

Today's Thought:

The saying goes, "Tell me who your friends are, and I'll tell you who you're becoming." Just like company dictates direction, company also determines success. There is no way you can build a house by yourself. You need the help of a foreman to lead the construction crew, you need plumbers and electricians. Even if you knew how to do all three trades, you would still need someone to come, inspect the property and make sure that the building is sound and safe to live in.

The verse today speaks about the importance of surrounding yourself with the right people. People that are willing to agree with the purpose of God for your life and not agree that it can't or won't happen. The book of Matthew tells us that there is significant power in agreement. You can come into agreement with someone else and cause things to move, shake and change. Be careful of people who pose as though they agree but are just really gathering intel for the day you potentially fail. Make sure you do share your faith and purpose with others, but make sure that those people are actually praying for you and keeping you accountable to your goals and dreams. Trust me, a mature person can tell when someone is in it for the benefits and not in it just to see someone succeed. There are others that will pray for you, but also sabotage your success if it means that they cannot be a part of the end goal or get a platform out of it.

Surround yourself with the right team of people that don't think like you do, but also have the same goal in mind as you. True friends like that cannot be duplicated or replaced. You shouldn't be the smartest person in your circle. There is something you can always learn from others, even when you've known them for a long time. If the friends you had around are no longer there, thank God that they left. Maybe God was protecting you from a possible distraction or derailment to the purpose that He has designed for you. The foreman's job is not to criticize the design, but to make sure that the blueprint becomes a reality. So today, rest assured that every enemy has been defeated and that as long as you surround yourself with the right people, whatever you have agreed upon, God will include himself in that and bless it.

Today's Declaration:

Lord, today I thank you for sending the right people to my life. I also thank you for removing those that are no longer around. You have protected me, and I thank you for that. Today, I pray for those that I need in my life and I thank you for the power of agreement. I also pray for those people that I need in my life that I haven't met yet. I thank you because you will send them just when I need them.

In Jesus name, Amen!

Day 4 – No Shortcuts

Today's Scripture: Matthew 7:13 (NKJV)

[13] *"Enter by the narrow gate; for wide is the gate and broad is the way that leads to destruction, and there are many who go in by it.*

Today's Thought:

Naturally, the logical way is always the easy way. Our minds are wired to think that there is always an easier way out. Psychiatrists will agree that your mind will hide from trouble when it senses a situation will be difficult. In other words, the mind will avoid a situation if it feels danger or feels it cannot come out on the winning end.

When building, you cannot take any shortcuts. When building a table, you can't get to the end and say that all the extra screws left behind where just because "it came with extras." When building, it requires precision and ensuring that what you've built will stand the test of time. When you follow the plan, there is no room for extras. There is no room for extras because what God has for you is custom built and doesn't come with spares. There is no space for carelessness. That's why during the first few days, we focused on the character requirements, and then got to picking up the hammer and working on this thing.

There is a saying that goes, "What doesn't start right, doesn't end right." This proved the fact that you can build the tallest building in the world, but if you took shortcuts and didn't set up its foundation correctly, it's just a matter of time before that building comes crashing down. God warns us of this in the book of Matthew because He knows that sometimes in our own immaturity, we can become careless in certain areas of our lives. We want to speed up the process and get to the end result without going through the proper steps. Our main job is to follow directions and follow His instructions on taking the road less traveled. This narrow gate doesn't just apply to our salvation, but it also applies to forgiving and loving others despite their many flaws. It also applies to forgiving ourselves, even when others can't seem to forgive you for what you have done in the past.

Today's Declaration:

Lord, today give me the grace to endure hardship. To go through the entire process, regardless of how I feel. Today, I vow to walk by faith and not by sight. As long as you walk me by the hand, I thank you that you will never lead me astray. Give me the grace to forgive others and to forgive myself. What you are building through me will stand the test of time because I'm going to go through the entire process, and I am not going to take any shortcuts.

In Jesus name, Amen.

Day 5 – Structure

Today's Scripture: 1 Corinthians 14:39-40 (NKJV)

[39] Therefore, brethren, desire earnestly to prophesy, and do not forbid to speak with tongues. [40] Let all things be done decently and in order.

Today's Thought:

Structure and organization work hand-in-hand. Paul writes to the church of Corinth in this text to let them know that although you have the gifts and gifted people in your church, there should still be structure and order. This also applies to our time and day. You can have the best job in the world, but if you don't have structure in your life and if you're not organized, the odds are that you will lose that job and find it difficult to be successful. All because you don't know how to set things in their proper order.

Structure also means that you have to prioritize. People have come to me and told me the different orders that they have their lives in. Not one is wrong, as long as God is the center and beginning of your plans. True order starts with God, family, then everything else. My family comes first before ministry. I have heard of people who have lost their families because they spend more time in church than they do with their own children. Now, I am not saying to completely abandon your church and fellowship life with believers. I am saying that you have to create order and structure. Structure is significant because this is what your children are going to model after. Unfortunately, many people live chaotic lives because they were not modeled structure in their childhood, so they birthed chaos in their adulthood. This is where you need to create a new pattern of order for your children to model after. Your children do not become what you say, they become what you do. It's never too late to pattern structure and order. Just like a parent that is willing to help their children put away the toys, God loves to help His children when they need the grace to bring structure and order to their lives.

When building, structure is necessary, especially when working with heavy and costly materials. Bring structure to your prayers because your prayers carry weight and can carry you through your day and week. Always start your day with thanksgiving and end it with thanksgiving. A grateful heart is one that can never be contaminated with selfishness and greed. As long as your prayers remain structured in thought with thanksgiving at the helm, there is nothing that can throw off your day and week.

Today's Declaration:

Lord, today I thank you for new structure in my life. Thank you because you are reminding me of the important things in my life, and you are giving me the grace to prioritize them. Give me the grace and confidence to cut and remove the things that are not important in this season of my life. Just like you did in Genesis, you spoke order, and so will I.

In Jesus name, Amen.

Day 6 – Framework

Today's Scripture: Hebrews 11:1-3 (NKJV)

11 Now faith is the substance of things hoped for, the evidence of things not seen. ²For by it the elders obtained a good testimony.

³ By faith we understand that the worlds were framed by the word of God, so that the things which are seen were not made of things which are visible.

Today's Thought:

If you had the choice to frame a house with plastic tubing or with wood, which would you choose? I would also choose wood. Wood is a much stronger material that can withstand weight, pressure and the wear that time takes on anything. This is the same perspective that we have on the words that God spoke from the very beginning of creation. Hebrews shows us that the worlds were framed by His word. All He had to say was a couple words, and there it was. Our world is a reflection of the words that come out of our mouths. You are what you say about yourself. If you say that it won't happen, it won't happen. If you say that it's impossible, then it's impossible.

Our words become the framework of our lives and sustain the relationships we carry. The words of today frame the world of tomorrow. This is why Dr. Martin Luther King Jr. delivered the "I have a dream" speech in

August of 1963. The following year, children all around the United States of America were affected by the Civil Rights Act of 1964. His words broke segregation laws that were in place for years before anyone said anything.

Wisdom teaches you that you don't have to say everything that is on your mind. Sometimes the best thing to do is to be quiet and wait for things to play out. If you've seen or have been in a court proceeding, a judge doesn't deliver their verdict immediately. They listen to both sides of the story, the defense and the prosecution. Time tells all and silence gives you time to think and analyze. Rather than spoil it with what you say, learn to be silent and not affect your future with the careless words that might slip out. Most of us have to be like small children again. We have to learn how to talk the right way. Next time you feel like saying something out of spite, hold your tongue and don't respond. Give yourself some time to think about your response, pray to see if it's the wisest thing to do, and then act. Your words carry power. Use that power to build, not to destroy.

Today's Declaration:

Lord, today I declare that I will guard my tongue. Thank you for wisdom of words and how to frame them properly. Today, I ask for the grace to speak up when I have to speak up, and to remain silent when I have to remain silent. Today, I will change my world with the words that come from my mouth. I will frame a world of peace, love, joy and health today with my words. Let it be my mouth but fill it with your words.

In Jesus name, Amen.

Day 7 – Insulate

Today's Scripture: Psalm 27:1-4 (NKJV)

27
The Lord is my light and my salvation;
Whom shall I fear?
The Lord is the strength of my life;
Of whom shall I be afraid?
2
When the wicked came against me
To eat up my flesh,
My enemies and foes,
They stumbled and fell.
3
Though an army may encamp against me,
My heart shall not fear;
Though war may rise against me,
In this I will be confident.
4
One thing I have desired of the Lord,
That will I seek:
That I may dwell in the house of the Lord
All the days of my life,
To behold the beauty of the Lord,
And to inquire in His temple.

Today's Thought:

If you live in a cold climate like I do, you know the importance of good insulation. You come into your house from zero-degree temperatures with freezing wind chill, in a good insulated house, you can feel the warmth of the furnace bring life back to your [almost] frostbitten skin. In that same climate, you will definitely appreciate the insulation of a good coat to cover you with and lessen your exposure to frostbite. Insulation doesn't just keep outside elements out, but it also makes sure that your heater isn't heating the entire neighborhood and seeping out somewhere; it keeps everything in.

These verses written by David remind us today that there is no better place than to be insulated and covered in God's house and in His presence. That even though enemies come against you, you have no reason to fear because He is covering you. In the same way, insulating our lives is making sure that what God has put in us, doesn't go wasted because we didn't know how to insulate and properly protect the gifts that God has given us. Some of the most gifted people I know are sometimes over-worked, under-paid, and tired of their jobs. They are tired of always giving and never getting anything in return. This is also a trend within many pastors and ministry leaders in the body of Christ. You find that many of them are tired and frustrated with ministry because they have been overworked.

A greater level of commitment to ministry and to Christ requires a greater level of stewardship. Why? Because you can't go to church every day of the week. You can't be in every ministry of the church, although you love to participate in what's going on in your local church. You can't pray twenty-four hours a day. We have to learn how to manage our time and prioritize what's important to us. You make time for what's important to you. That also means that you have to be aware of the people who are constantly trying take your time and breaking into the insulation that you have placed in the walls of your house. These people constantly need a handout, want your attention, and don't know how to make a decision without consulting someone for their opinion. I've learned to always take things to God in prayer, even if it's a small decision to make. I believe God finds pleasure in His children including Him in every area of their lives. I've also learned to trust my judgement and my instinct in other situations. Learn to trust what you know to be right and always know that God won't lead you where His hand can't keep you. Protect yourself and guard yourself, but also know that His angels have been assigned to cover you and your loved ones.

Today's Declaration:

Lord, today allow me to discern the things that are depleting me of my strength and my commitment to living my best life. Today, I ask for the strength and courage to bind people's opinions of me and judgements. Allow me to always be mindful and make it priority to live in your house. Thank you for right relationships that will help insulate and keep my fire alive and well.

In Jesus name, Amen.

Day 8 – Grace

Today's Scripture: 2 Corinthians 9:8 (NKJV)

8 And God is able to make all grace abound toward you, that you, always having all sufficiency in all things, may have an abundance for every good work.

Today's Thought:

Every day requires a fresh amount of grace. If you live a busy life like me, you know you need it as fresh as He can give it. As the children of Israel would ask for their daily bread, it was a fresh manifestation of grace that they were really asking for. They knew that they didn't deserve it because of their disobedience, but they also knew that the God they served was a God full of mercy and rich in love. Many times, we don't have because we don't ask. I constantly have to look to Him and remember that He finished the work, and if I am in need of it, He is able to come through.

God, as a Father, loves His children. Paul tells us that in the many years of his life and ministry, he never saw the righteous forsaken. This tells me that grace and mercy are never-ending to them that have believed in Him and have now been called His children. One thing to note is that although God loves everyone, not everyone loves

Him. It's not about loving God to the measure that He loves us, because that would be impossible. But it's having the confidence that when you call, He will answer. It's knowing that He is able to make a way where there is no way.

My father is an incredible man. I consider him my hero in many ways. In times where my car stopped working, I've called my dad before to give me a ride to drop off the car at the repair shop. I wouldn't even bother him if I knew he couldn't do it. I only ask him because I know that he is able to help. The same way I know my dad is able to do, I know that my heavenly Father is able. The fact that I pray and ask Him is the validation that is He able to do it. Some people ask, but don't think He's able. It's like asking my dad for a ride but asking him how he is going to do it. If I ask Him, I might not know how He's going to do it, but I know He's able to do it. According to John, one of His characteristics is that He is "The Way." That means that He is an expert in making a way where there is no way. And because His other characteristic is that He is a builder, before He created me, He made a way. He had the end in mind before the beginning. Your Plan B is His Plan A. Before there was a problem, He had made the solution. If I call on His grace to see me through the building effort, it will be available to me when I call on it.

Today's Declaration:

Lord, today I acknowledge that you have provided for me a new day and a new grace. I know you to be faithful and able to do more than what I can ask for. Even though you can surpass my imagination, I still ask you to surprise me today. Open doors that are impossible for me to open, and close doors that are impossible for me to close. As I ask, I also trust that you're providing in all directions and in all areas of my life where I need it the most.

In Jesus name, Amen.

Day 9 – The Covering

Today's Scripture: Psalms 91:1-2 (NKJV)

1 *He who dwells in the secret place of the Most High Shall abide under the shadow of the Almighty.*[2] *I will say of the Lord, "He is my refuge and my fortress; My God, in Him I will trust.*

Today's Thought:

A roof on a house is one of the most important things to consider during construction. What is the point of putting in new walls and expensive lumber, if any type of weather can get in? You would be wasting valuable money if you haven't invested in a good roof to shelter the investment made inside of house. Walls speak to lateral intruders (thieves, animals, etc.), and roofs speak to horizontal enemies such as storms and things that sometimes cannot be controlled. You can't control if it rains or not, but you can choose to put a new roof on for the next time it does rain.

Sometimes the enemy attacks us by sending storms our way that we didn't expect. Sometimes, it's not the enemy, and it's just life. David encountered several storms in his life. The one thing he knew he had was the covering of his heavenly Father. The storms in life can come all they want, but I know who I've placed my trust in. God's hand of protection doesn't have an expiration date. David refers to Him as a refuge and a fortress that cannot be penetrated. Although the enemy comes with everything he has, it's still not enough when compared to the army of angels that cover me and my family. For this reason, I sleep in peace every night. I have no worries if it's going to rain or not. Why? Because I'm covered and everything that is connected to me is covered. In New York we have snow. Snow doesn't worry me, either. Come what may, I cannot be touched because I'm covered.

Today's focus is really being at peace. Many people are constantly stressed out because they're afraid something is going to happen or they're always under attack. To me, that is the definition of anxiety. It hasn't happened yet, but just the possibility of it happening makes you anxious, won't let you sleep and won't let you eat. I've learned to rest in the victory of Jesus Christ. His grace produces rest in me that cannot be overcome. Do situations still come? Do storms still arise? Yes. But now, I have something I didn't have when I started building. I have true shelter that keeps me from the elements in life I cannot control.

Today's Declaration:

Lord, today I thank you for the covering that you are. You are a strong tower where I can run and be safe.

Today, I ask that you take all the pressure off and anxiety away. I declare that I will rest in your protection and know that nothing happens in my life that you have not seen or allowed. I will live and conquer this day with boldness and all fear of tomorrow and what will come must go now!

In Jesus name, Amen.

Day 10 – No More Cycles

Today's Scripture: Isaiah 43:19 (NKJV)

9

Behold, I will do a new thing,
Now it shall spring forth;
Shall you not know it?
I will even make a road in the wilderness
And rivers in the desert.

Today's Thought:

What makes a pregnant woman pregnant? Is the fact that she told everyone that she is now expecting cause pregnancy? A seed. Because the woman received a seed, her normal cycle stops. This is the reason why when the woman with the issue of blood came to Jesus, the cycle ended. She came in contact with the seed of Abraham (Galatians 3:16) and that made the cycle of sickness in her life come to a close. And the Prophet Isaiah says the same thing in this text to us today. That God is doing something new, which means that He is breaking the old patterns in our lives.

Cycles are typically generational patterns and personal patterns that don't allow us to move on in what God has called for us to do with our lives. For example, cycles can be an addiction to drugs, pornography or habitual lying that cannot be broken. It can also be a cycle of old patterns of thinking, being in bad relationships that have no long-term value, and it seems like you engage in a relationship with one bad person after another. It feels like in every situation, you get the shorter end of the stick and just can't shake it.

In starting this devotional, you might have just broken a cycle in your own life. The fact that you started and intend on finishing it might have broken a pattern in your bloodline of people that constantly start something and never finish. For some, just starting it was part of a broken cycle in your life. His grace and the power of His blood breaks every cycle. It means that just because your father was an alcoholic, doesn't mean you have to be an alcoholic. Just because no one in your family ever graduated from college, doesn't mean you won't. Divorce doesn't have to be the end of your marriage, just because it was the case for your parents.

Whether you're trying to build on your self-esteem, on your family or career, know that from this point on, all cycles in your life of failure have come to an end. Success is eminent if you stay committed to the dream and the blueprint.

Today's Declaration:

Lord, thank you for birthing and starting something new in my life. Today, I declare a new pattern in springing up in my thoughts and actions. The things I used to think, don't have control of me anymore. The failure and defeat I used to feel, I let go of right now. As I start this new day, I also start a new pattern of thought wrapped in what you said about me and not what I think about myself.

In Jesus name, Amen.

Day 11 – Power

Today's Scripture: 1 Corinthians 2:1-5 (NKJV)

1 And I, brethren, when I came to you, did not come with excellence of speech or of wisdom declaring to you the testimony of God. 2 For I determined not to know anything among you except Jesus Christ and Him crucified. 3 I was with you in weakness, in fear, and in much trembling. 4 And my speech and my preaching were not with persuasive words of human[b] wisdom, but in demonstration of the Spirit and of power, 5 that your faith should not be in the wisdom of men but in the power of God.

Today's Thought:

Power is real and can be felt. Ever sat in a really fast car? Have you ever been shocked by a power outlet when plugging something in? Because an object possesses a certain amount of power, whatever comes into contact with it will feel its power and be affected by it. The same way power works with a car or a battery, a greater amount of power has been deposited in you by the Holy Spirit. This power has a way of breaking habits, bad attitudes, casting depression off, anxiety lifts and it gives a supernatural strength to do what you can't do in your own strength. If this power is truly working in you, those things and people that surround you, have to be affected and influenced by it. This power also activates a supernatural grace to overcome what you weren't able to overcome on your own. His strength isn't perfected in your strength. His strength can only be perfected in your weakness. Because you can't do it yourself, is not a bad thing; it's actually a good thing.

During construction, all the power lines are installed to provide light and power throughout the house. This way, anything that connected to that resource of power such as an outlet, can do what it was designed to do. A vacuum is useless if it hasn't been connected to a source of power. A television wouldn't work if it isn't connected to a source of power. Just like outlets are designed to be a resource of power, you have been designed and fashioned in this world to be a resource of power. Everyone around that is not living to their God-given purpose, once they connect to you, will begin to function purposely and properly.

You can't always see power lines in a house. They are hidden behind walls and underground. The power can't be seen from the outside. But you better believe that when it's manifested, it can be felt and will begin to revive the [once] dead things around me.

Today's Declaration:

Lord, today I declare that I carry your power and might. I refuse to let what I feel determine what I possess. If your

Spirit lives within me, your power also lives within me. I declare that the same power that lives in me is the same power that rose Jesus from the grave. Today, it is going to resurrect every dead dream and vision that I had for my life. You have not made me weak, but powerful through your Holy Spirit. Allow me to demonstrate that power wherever I go.

In Jesus name, Amen.

Day 12 – Strength

Today's Scripture: Psalms 28:7 (NLT)

The Lord is my strength and shield.
I trust him with all my heart.
He helps me, and my heart is filled with joy.
I burst out in songs of thanksgiving.

Today's Thought:

What is the source of your strength? What keeps you motivated? What makes you wake up in the morning? Power and strength, although they are synonymous, they have different functions. If you think of a Wi-Fi connection, although the Wi-Fi connection has been powered, if the signal doesn't have enough strength, you cannot connect to the internet. Although the Holy Spirit gives you power, if you don't ask God for His strength, what seems to be small will become extremely significant and overwhelming. Although you have the power to overcome, some don't have the strength to fight when the opposition arises.

Some years ago, I counseled a couple that was married for about five years. They came to my wife and I looking for counseling because we had expressed our availability to help others within the local church. During the meeting, the wife expressed her disappointment in her husband in his unwillingness to yield to the call over his life. She said something that until this day, still rings within me. She said that although she loved him and didn't want to leave him, she was just tired of fighting for them both. This example showed me that although the Holy Spirit gives you the power to overcome personal battles and to obtain victory over situations, you really need God's strength to wait on Him to do what He said He would do.

Again, all the power has been given to us. Now all we need is His strength to wait on Him. As you know, some blessings and victories are progressive. Not all financial and health prayers are answered instantaneously. This is why David said He will give strength to those that wait on Him. His strength truly shines when delay and waiting is involved. Although difficult to understand in the moment, delay reveals the hand of God in the situation. How? Because in retrospect you can look at a few scenarios and situations in your life where God delayed things intentionally. If He hadn't delayed them, you could have risked derailing it by getting ahead of schedule and getting ahead of your growth at the time. Additionally, the delay revealed that only God was able to do what He did. You were out of money, resources and ideas, and that's when He came through. Like a basketball player in the clutch with the winning shot, He made it just in time. Take every delay in your life as an opportunity for His strength to be developed in and through you.

Today's Declaration:

Lord, today I thank you for being my strength and sustainer. Thank you for keeping me in the most difficult times of my life and for keeping me when I don't fully understand what is going on. I also thank you for delay, because it is shaping me and making me stronger, wiser and more mature. I trust that you are going to make all things happen in their time.

In Jesus name, Amen.

Day 13 – Boarders

Today's Scripture: Nehemiah 3:4-6 (NKJV)

4 Then the king said to me, "What do you request?"
So I prayed to the God of heaven. 5 And I said to the
king, "If it pleases the king, and if your servant has found
favor in your sight, I ask that you send me to Judah, to
the city of my fathers 'tombs, that I may rebuild it."
6 Then the king said to me (the queen also sitting beside
him), "How long will your journey be? And when will you
return?" So it pleased the king to send me; and I set him
a time.

Today's Thought:

One of the most important components of a house are the
walls. Walls not only cover the imperfections of the
wood framing set in place, but it also divides the outside
of the house and the inside of the house. If a house
doesn't have walls, any person or animal and come right
in. Walls speak to the boarders we have to set up in our
lives. Some people think that putting up walls is a bad
thing, as if you put them up to isolate yourself. I'm
referring to the importance of putting up boarders to
protect and make sure that people aren't just taking
advantage of your goodness and your family. Not
everyone has your best interest in mind. Even the United
States has boarders. They set them to make sure that

people don't just come into this country without having the proper authorization to do so. If you come in illegally, you are subject to deportation. Many of us, have to do the same exact thing. Those that trespass the boarders and boundaries we have set in place, need to be checked and we have to make sure we can trust them before we hand them the keys to our lives.

If you read the book of Nehemiah, he felt a great responsibility to rebuild the walls of Jerusalem after enemies had come and overtaken the city. Boarders speak about protection to your citizens, your way of doing things and even your economic stability. As soon as those walls came down, so did all those factors. When you don't set boundaries, even in relationships, you make yourself vulnerable to whatever the other person considers good friendship. You have to set boundaries because you when you set boarders and boundaries, you set expectations for others and for yourself. This will avoid being let down and setting expectations that others cannot meet.

Today's Declaration:

Lord, today I will build the right walls in my life. Today I tear down every wall of isolation and rebuild walls of importance and protection in my life. As of today, I will no longer allow people to come into my life illegally and rule my decisions or cloud my judgement. Thank you for giving me a new heart to protect the treasure you've left in me.

In Jesus name, Amen.

Day 14 – Let Go!

Today's Scripture: Hebrews 12:1 (NLV)

1 All these many people who have had faith in God are around us like a cloud. Let us put every thing out of our lives that keeps us from doing what we should. Let us keep running in the race that God has planned for us. 2 Let us keep looking to Jesus. Our faith comes from Him and He is the One Who makes it perfect. He did not give up when He had to suffer shame and die on a cross. He knew of the joy that would be His later. Now He is sitting at the right side of God.

Today's Thought:

Before we get to the half-way point, I call this the evaluation checkpoint. This is the place where you have to check yourself and see if there is anything in you that has or can potentially hold you back. Experience teaches you that sometimes people hold you back, mistakes hold you back and even previous success can hold you back. This is a great place to look back and thank God for everything that you've gone through. This is imperative. Looking back gives you a better perspective towards the future. Experience wouldn't be experience if you didn't go through it. A good relationship isn't really defined clearly to you unless you've been in a bad one. Retrospect gives you a snapshot of where you've come from, but you also have to keep your eyes looking forward.

Now that you've looked back and thanked God the experience or season, let it go! I think this is probably one of the top things that I find as a constant in counseling with couples. The previous relationship wasn't the best, so now the good guy or girl that comes along becomes the perpetrator. Many relationships fail because some people don't know how to let go of what once was. Yes, you have to look back and learn from that experience. But the point of that experience is to move on. After hitting rock bottom, there is nowhere to go but up. If your rock bottom was bankruptcy, learn the financial lesson from it and move on. If your rock bottom was a failed marriage, learn from the things that contributed to that divorce and move on. If your rock bottom was a lay off from a job that you thought you would eventually retire from, learn from it and move on. Some of the worst experiences in my life taught me my greatest lessons. Many times, you will be faced with that decision again. If not, you will encounter someone in your life that is going to go through something similar. What will be your answer or advice? That is the part where the student becomes the teacher. The point of an open book test is not to prove whether you are smart or not. The point of an open book test is to prove that you know the material and you know where to find the answer.

When faced with trouble, look back to see how you got out, and move on! Planes don't have a reverse gear and God's children shouldn't either. We are meant to go back, but with the purpose to be launched forward.

Today's Declaration:

Lord, today I thank you for this place of reflection. Thank you for every hill and valley. Thank you for every lesson and test that I didn't want to take because it taught me something about myself. I cannot and will not go back to where I used to be, but I will press forward and go higher into the places where you have called for me to go.

In Jesus name, Amen.

Day 15 – Take Inventory

Today's Scripture: John 6:11-12 (NKJV)

11 *And Jesus took the loaves, and when He had given thanks He distributed them to the disciples, and the disciples[a] to those sitting down; and likewise of the fish, as much as they wanted.* **12** *So when they were filled, He said to His disciples, "Gather up the fragments that remain, so that nothing is lost."*

Today's Thought:

Where do we go from here? You learned and you moved on. The important thing before moving forward in any project is always taking inventory of what you have left and what you need to complete the job at hand. These last few days have been extremely important to your personal growth. Today, you are halfway through construction. It's also an important day because you don't have as many materials left around now, compared to when you nailed the first pieces of wood together.

I constantly travel with my pen and pad in hand. Sometimes, I feel like God is talking to me the entire day. I don't like to miss a thing because it could be the word that I need as an answer for a prayer I've had. As a foreman takes notes of materials used and materials needed, this is a great place to write down what you need to finish the task at hand. Who you need to complete the task ahead and what you've learned so far will serve as a benefit for the next half.

You don't want to get near the finish line and say that you forgot to get something. That always slows you down and impedes those that have been sent to your life to help you. If you don't know that you need to finish, how can they help? What tools do you need? These are the resources needed to complete the job. This could consist of looking at your financial budget and making sure that you're still on track to buy that house you've always wanted. As Jesus asked His disciples to gather up the fragments, you also have to gather up what is left after you feel you've started one of the greatest projects of your life. Don't let anything go to waste and see what you can still use. I'm sure that you can still build something with those pieces of wood that were left over. They might be cut, but they aren't damaged. This is the importance of taking inventory of the great and true friends that we have in our lives. They might have messed up, but they are still your friends. Access the reality that an opportunity like this doesn't happen every day and that you will finish what you started.

Today's Declaration:

Lord, today I thank you for every single thing in my life right now. From the small things to the things that I consider to be big. I thank you because I will not take for granted anything that you have done in my life. Today, allow me to gather the things and people that I have placed to the side and lost importance for. Give me insight as to their place in my life and their role in this next season.

In Jesus name, Amen.

Day 16 – Replenish and Recharge

Today's Scripture: Galatians 6:9 (NKJV)

9 And let us not grow weary while doing good, for in due season we shall reap if we do not lose heart.

Today's Thought:

Now that you've taken inventory, it's time to replenish. Since we are past the half-way mark, this is the point where many find themselves with not enough strength to continue. Some are known for starting something and not finishing it. Maybe it was the kitchen remodel, or the spring-cleaning project. Either way, learn to take a break before you start this again. I'm not referring to an extended vacation. I'm referring to taking a break from work, enjoying your family, enjoy the weather and be present.

Yes, it's important to keep focus on the task at hand. But it's also important to stop, breathe and relax for a moment. Replenish means to fill up again. What good is a brand-new car if the tank is empty? Although we've taken inventory and seen what we need to finish, we also have to consider the energy we need to finish what we've started. Learn to just take a day for yourself. If you have a family, take the kids out to the movies or treat them to some ice cream. I believe everyone who works hard, deserves a vacation or staycation. You deserve to take some time off and enjoy the sunlight or the snow.

At home, I'm known as dad. My children are so young that they don't know what I do for a living and I'm sure they don't care. What they will remember is the time I spent with them and the good laughs that we had. My wife always asks me about my day, but there are days when I don't dwell on my workday because I'm just glad I'm home. Whichever way you are able to unplug and replenish, do it. This time will not be wasted and will help immensely for the hard days to come. People faint because they ran out of fuel and cannot continue. There is a due harvest with your name on it, but you have to make sure you fuel up and stay in the game to see this thing through.

Today's Declaration:

Lord, today I thank you for replenishing my strength for the days to come. Although there is much work to be done, I focus on today and take it one day at a time. Allow me to always keep perspective that you are the source of my strength and my deliverer. If I ever feel like fainting or giving up, I thank you in advance because you will replenish my strength.

In Jesus name, Amen.

Day 17 – Give It All You Have

Today's Scripture: Matthew 26:6-9 (NKJV)

6 And when Jesus was in Bethany at the house of Simon the leper, 7 a woman came to Him having an alabaster flask of very costly fragrant oil, and she poured it on His head as He sat at the table. 8 But when His disciples saw it, they were indignant, saying, "Why this waste? 9 For this fragrant oil might have been sold for much and given to the poor."

Today's Thought:

Let's get these engines running again! You've moved past the replenish and recharge stage, and now have to pick up that hammer and keep working. Although replenishing your supply took some work, this next half we tend to feel lazy and sluggish, but instead let's keep moving forward. Sometimes, you wake up, and things just feel out of whack. Some people resort to coffee every day to function, some resort to working out to get the energy for the day, others take vitamins. Every single day is an opportunity to get closer to the destiny and the call that God has designed for your life.

The woman with the alabaster box poured all she had at the feet of Jesus. Historians believe that she had taken her one year's wages to pay for this box of costly perfume. As soon as she poured it out, the disciples themselves criticized her and were boggled as to why she would waste such costly perfume. To others, what you're doing might be a waste of time. Those are people that you should not spend your time with. What you think is an investment, they think is a waste. Value is not proportionate to what it's worth. Value is proportionate to what someone is willing to pay for it. To some, the time you're spending on improving your marriage may be a waste, but it's really an investment. To some, spending time in church or having a relationship with God may be a waste. It's really an eternal investment.

Now that we know it's an investment, we have to give this all we have. You have to commit yourself to this project. An investment is spending time with your family, taking your spouse on a date, coming up with more ideas to get your business off the ground or volunteering at your church. Why? Because it's worth more than what others value it at. It's all a matter of perspective and giving it all you have, even when you're the only one that believes it.

Today's Declaration:

Lord, today I thank you for the strength and resilience you've given me in this process. Give me the grace not to focus on what people are saying, but to focus on the task at hand. With my life, you can have everything that belongs to me. Everything that I have is yours. Give me a better perspective and allow me to value the things that are important and the things that I want to see grow and flourish in my life.

In Jesus name, Amen.

Day 18 – Focus

Today's Scripture: Hebrews 12:2 (GNT)

2 Let us keep our eyes fixed on Jesus, on whom our faith depends from beginning to end. He did not give up because of the cross! On the contrary, because of the joy that was waiting for him, he thought nothing of the disgrace of dying on the cross, and he is now seated at the right side of God's throne.

Today's Thought:

Because we are going to give it all we have, we need to focus. Focus is the enemy of distraction. As soon as you have focused in on a particular project, distraction will rear its ugly head and try to take your eyes off of the prize. A motivated individual is powerful, but a focused individual is even mightier. As you know, several states have passed laws against texting while driving. Why? Because texting shifts the driver's focus off the road where it should be. Focus isn't easy to accomplish, especially when you have a million things going through your mind and things to do in one day. This is the same focus that Jesus asked Peter to have when he was trying to walk on water.

The writer of Hebrews reminds us that we have to literally fix and keep our eyes on Jesus, who has authored our lives. To the common man, this makes no sense because why would you surrender control of your life to someone who you can't see? That's what faith is all about. It's knowing that the God that lives in you was already in your past and already knows your tomorrow.

Eagles have incredible vision. Research has shown that they can spot an animal in the grass from the sky almost 2 miles away. That requires focus. This is the same focus that we need when tackling things every day. Although there are one hundred plus things going on around us, we have to focus and fix our eyes on Jesus, because He will lead us unto all truth and provide us with supernatural focus to see what others seem to be distracted from. Just keep your eyes on Jesus, and you will be able to excel in the things that other people seem to fail at.

Today's Declaration:

Lord, today give me the focus of an eagle. Allow me to focus on the things that are important and let me let go of the things that cannot give me life. Thank you because nothing is impossible, as long as I keep my eyes on you. I come against the things that are not important that are trying to get my attention and declare that I will not be distracted another day by them.

In Jesus name, Amen.

Day 19 – Open Windows

Today's Scripture: Malachi 3:10 (NKJV)

Bring all the tithes into the storehouse,
That there may be food in My house,
And try Me now in this,"
Says the Lord of hosts,
"If I will not open for you the windows of heaven
And pour out for you such blessing
That there will not be room enough to receive it.

Today's Thought:

During construction, it's important to open the windows. By opening the windows, I'm not allowing dust to settle inside the property. After some time, things can begin to accumulate. After the wood has been cut, you can see even more dust spread inside.

By opening windows, we are saying that two things can happen; something can get out and something can get in. As it relates to our lives, open windows mean that we are ready to let something out. Have you ever overcooked food and the smoke begins to cloud the house? The first thing that you do is run to the window and open it to get all the smoke out. It also serves as an emergency exit to get out in the case of a fire. Now, when summer arrives and it's extremely hot inside your house, the same thing is done to cool down your home.

Malachi tells us that if we test God in our giving, He would open a supernatural window of provision in our lives. We trust God with everything in our lives. One of the things that needs to be sorted out during the building up of a family or the repair of a marriage is the financial situation. This seems to be the common denominator when we look at statistics for divorce. We also see that money was a contributing factor when the prodigal son left the home of his father. Before he left, he asked the father for his share of the inheritance. The way that we keep open windows in our lives is by giving. Giving frees you from the spirit of greed and of being self-serving. You don't have to be monetarily compensated for everything that you do to help others.

Money is not everything but will be one of the greatest tests of your life. Whether today, tomorrow or someday, you will be tested with money. This test will reveal your true position as it relates to greed. This could be the loss of a job or an unexpected expense. At the same time, God will see if you are still committed to giving and loving others the same way you did when the bank account was full. Many times, we will find ourselves in financial frustration and take it out on our spouses. We have to learn to love, in-spite of the economic circumstance. If you have lost it all, as long as you have God, you have it all. Our source has been and will always be God.

Today's Declaration:

Lord, today I thank you that money has no rulership over my life. You are a provider and a keeper. In the same way that you provided for Abraham when it appeared that there was no other way, thank you because you will do the same with me and mine. Today, I declare you are opening the windows of heaven over my life and over my future generations.

In Jesus name, Amen.

Day 20 – Closed Doors

Today's Scripture: Matthew 6:6 (NKJV)

6 *But you, when you pray, go into your room, and when you have shut your door, pray to your Father who is in the secret place; and your Father who sees in secret will reward you openly.*

Today's Thought:

At the end of the night, you don't leave your doors open for just anyone to walk in. You've invested a great deal of money, time and effort into this project. Doors symbolize access. People don't have access to your property unless they have given them keys to your doors. Jesus reminds us in today's scripture that when we go before the Father, we have to close the door behind us.

The enemy comes and gives us a great deal of trouble because someone left the door open somewhere. Thieves don't usually come through the front door, but they always check the back door to see if someone might have left it open by mistake. Open doors can consist of secrets that you keep to yourself and that you haven't wanted to share with your spouse or with a friend to be accountable. An open door can also be an unresolved conflict or not healing from an abuse that occurred in your childhood or youth. These doors have always been the first place where the enemy comes to check and see if that has been dealt with. If not, the enemy will provide you with alternatives that can ultimately lead to the end of a relationship, a marriage, or the separation of your family. I've seen in the past where a spouse has kept a secret from the other, and after many years invested in their marriage, it ends in divorce because they had a weakness or suffered something in their childhood that finally came to light and devastated the marriage to a place they believed was irreparable.

At times, we have also left a door open because we've leant the keys of our heart to too many people. It's about that time that you get the keys back from everyone who has had access to your heart. This can be done by calling family members, anyone that has offended you or that you have offended and asking for forgiveness. You don't want to be right; you just want closure. You want to close the door. This could also be closing the chapter on certain relationships because the goal of growing and getting better is not mutual. Close the doors and make sure you check the locks twice before leaving for the day.

Today's Declaration:

Lord, today I vow to draw closer to you and close every door behind me. Thank you because your intent is to draw me closer to your presence and to your person. I declare that all thieves in my life must leave now and those that have trespassed must put back what they have stolen.

In Jesus name, Amen.

Day 21 – Answered Prayers

Today's Scripture: 1 John 5:14-15 (NKJV)

14 Now this is the confidence that we have in Him, that if we ask anything according to His will, He hears us. 15 And if we know that He hears us, whatever we ask, we know that we have the petitions that we have asked of Him.

Today's Thought:

Answered prayers usually come as a consequence of 3 things: Obedience to God's will, God's sovereignty, and the fact that you are His child. Today's verse tells us that He hears us when we pray. We have to focus on the fact that He hears us. At this point of your project, I know you've invested a significant amount of time in prayer asking God to lead you in certain areas and to also open doors in certain areas. My focus is not so much the prayers that have gone up but waiting on the reply to come back.

I've learned that during the construction process, I have to thank God for the distance He has brought me. When you are still waiting on Him to answer you concerning a matter, the Bible tells us that we should begin to think on things that are praiseworthy, things that are pure, things that are lovely and of a good report (Philippians 4:8). Although the project isn't completed, thank God that you've started and that you are going to see it through. This applies to your health and to your finances. Even when the situation doesn't look good and you are still waiting for God to perform His will, begin to think on the prayers that He has answered and the times that He has seen you through some of the darkest places in your life.

I refuse to put my trust in someone that cannot come through for me. The fact that I ask is proof that I believe He can and will answer in the right time. Patience is conceived in the womb of delay. As human beings, we want God to work on our schedule instead of His perfect timing. My wife and I had trouble trying to conceive our first child, Isabella. We lost the first child and became very discouraged. When we stopped trying so hard to make it happen on our time, God gave us the miracle of conception. His time is perfect because when all we are able to see is our present, He sees the entire picture; the beginning and the end.

Today, we thank God for answered prayers and the fact that if you are building according to His blueprint, He will provide the clarity to the unclear parts in due time. Faith is the component needed to continue walking, although the entire picture is not clear to you yet.

Today's Declaration:

Lord, today I thank you for hearing my prayers. I believe that you have heard every single prayer that I prayed and that they do not fall on closed ears, because you are a God that loves and hears His children. Today, I ask that you would give me the faith to believe to receive what I have prayed for. Even if there is delay, I thank you because it is giving me the patience to endure until you manifest what you've promised.

In Jesus name, Amen.

Day 22 – Add Some Color

Today's Scripture: Romans 12:2 (NKJV)

2 And do not be conformed to this world, but be transformed by the renewing of your mind, that you may prove what is that good and acceptable and perfect will of God.

Today's Thought:

As my wife says, "A coat of paint can transform any room." Now that the walls are up and we are almost finished with construction, it's time to put some paint on the walls. Colors speak about personality. Psychologists have determined that the colors people wear speak about their personality. People that are outspoken and having a beaming personality, typically prefer to wear brighter colors that reflect exactly that. Introverts, because they don't like to be noticed, typically wear darker colors and colors that are not out of the norm. Colors are also used to communicate a message. If someone were to color in the outline of a sun, they would use a bright yellow. This yellow communicates to our minds words such as hope, happiness and optimism.

In referring to our project, it's time that we add some color to our house. If not talking about a physical house, although that may be something you're considering, but speaking about your mental and emotional house. Just as we added some colors to the walls of our home to bring a sense of change, we also have to do the same to our minds so that we can tell that something has and is still changing. How do you erase bad memories? The Holy Spirit helps you create new ones. God never likes to see His creation sad or depressed, but He loves to see them full of hope, possibility and expectation. Renew your mind by the power of His Word that never changes. The beauty is that it changes you in the process.

If adding color means changing the way you see certain things, that might just be it. If it means starting to go to the gym or getting a makeover, well that might be it too. I believe it's all according to what you personally feel might be the area of your life that needs some color. Spontaneity in a relationship adds plenty of color to the way the other person sees you. It means that you're usually one way, but you've chosen to change it up and little. My wife loves spontaneity just like many women that are trying to spice things up once it a while. I'm more the creature of habit. She has taught me to put some paint in those areas of my life. It may be through trying new foods, dressing differently, or just learning to smile more. Just because you have always done one thing the same way for a long time, doesn't mean that you cannot change. Change is a good thing, so welcome it when it knocks at the door.

Although changes are necessary, they aren't always instantaneous. This month, paint one area. Then for next month, consider which area of your life needs some color. I bet that once you decide which area needs it, as soon as someone walks into that room and sees that part of it, it will cause them to see you differently.

Today's Declaration:

Lord, today I choose to transform the way I live by the way I think. Today, I decide to erase the negative thoughts that have been in my mind for such a long time and focusing on You. Today I renew my thoughts and feelings about how everything will turn out. I am aware that not everything will be perfect, but I choose the realm of the impossible in which You are an expert.

In Jesus name, Amen.

Day 23 – Smoke Alarms

Today's Scripture: Proverbs 4:23 (NKJV)

Keep your heart with all diligence,
For out of it spring the issues of life.

Today's Thought:

You call the firefighters when there is smoke, not when the house is on fire. This is a reminder that if you need help, you don't wait until the last minute to look for it. Smoke alarms in a house speak about preparation. Not that you're expecting the house to go up in flames in a year, but if the event happens, you are prepared and have enough time to either put it out or get what you care most about out in time.

I once counseled a couple that was having many issues. Although they had been together for a while, one of them was having significant doubts about the relationship and they were not married yet. After several sessions and several attempts to get to the heart of the issue, one of the them confessed to having fallen out of love. Now, I am no proponent to breaking someone's heart, but I also don't condone staying in a relationship with someone just to make them happy when you're not. Of course the one that was fighting for the relationship was extremely upset when it finally came out of the other person's mouth. While they were sharing their frustration, I said to myself, "Didn't you see the warning signs? Didn't they seem distant to you?" This is why you install smoke alarms. The moment the smoke alarm picks up the hint of carbon monoxide, it will go off and make a noise no one can ignore.

Proverbs is teaching us today that we have to guard our hearts diligently. This means that you have to constantly put your emotions in check. You have to learn how to see warning signs in any relationship and have the confidence to share your heart with someone you care about if something doesn't seem right. God also surrounds us with gifted people such as family, friends, pastors and so many others that you can trust with sensitive information. This information is not shared with people who haven't proven trustworthiness. You have to learn to confide in people that have proven that they are a safe and if someone tries to break them for information, they will never compromise your friendship and trust.

Today's Declaration:

Lord, today I vow to protect my heart with all diligence. I refuse to allow just anyone to sow seed in my heart when you have total possession of it. My heart is yours and the rhythm of my heart beats to your voice. Thank you for preserving me, even when I didn't know what was going on. From now on, give me discernment to know when I love the wrong things that have occupied the space of my heart with the wrong affections.

In Jesus name, Amen.

Day 24 – New Furniture

Today's Scripture: Daniel 2:21-22 (NKJV)

21
And He changes the times and the seasons;
He removes kings and raises up kings;
He gives wisdom to the wise
And knowledge to those who have understanding.
22
He reveals deep and secret things;
He knows what is in the darkness,
And light dwells with Him.

Today's Thought:

Out with the old, in with the new! We see in today's scripture that God is the God that brings in new seasons and a new time for us. Because we have already let go of the past some days ago, we now move on to what God has before us. Now that we have let go, we have to fill back up. A house is not really complete without the furniture. These are the things that you fill your life with to unplug, kick back and relax once you've come home from a long day at work.

You don't pick the furniture the day that you move into the house. You go to the store before it's time to move in so that you can make sure that the measurements are good and that all of it is going to fit. Now that we have chosen to start fresh, it's time to choose what things you are going to have around in your space to trust and lean on. I believe meeting new people is a big part of it. People are like furniture because with the right people, you are able to relax, lean on, cry or laugh with when the moment presents itself. This could mean reaching out to people in your local church or within your community of believers that you can spend some time with and get to know a little better. You would be surprised how much you can learn from a person who has a different perspective. The right people can provide you with a perspective you can't see yourself and give the mirror of truth in love.

When checking out this furniture, test it out. Make sure that it's not just going to be reliable in the showroom when everyone sees it, but it's going to be functional when you take it back home and no one else is around. The past is the past. That means that the past deceit that you encountered, is no longer the case and those are no longer your friends. You don't bring the past into a new place that God has designed for you to enjoy to the fullest.

Today's Declaration:

Lord, thank you because today you are arranging new order and placing new things to fill my life. Thank you because once you enter my house, you don't leave it alone, but you fill the places you enter. Continue to fill my house until I no longer have room for foolishness, immaturity and unfruitfulness.

In Jesus name, Amen.

Day 25 – Protection

Today's Scripture: Psalms 121:3-8 (NKJV)

3
He will not allow your foot to be moved;
He who keeps you will not slumber.
4
Behold, He who keeps Israel
Shall neither slumber nor sleep.
5
The Lord is your keeper;
The Lord is your shade at your right hand.
6
The sun shall not strike you by day,
Nor the moon by night.
7
The Lord shall preserve you from all evil;
He shall preserve your soul.
8
The Lord shall preserve your going out and your coming in
From this time forth, and even forevermore.

Today's Thought:

What's the point in making the huge investment in the structure and in all the furniture, if you have no security system in place? Boundaries and walls are necessary, but so are security alarms. At this juncture, we aren't talking about set expectations on others or on yourself, but this is where we place complete and total dependency on God.

Through the first part of this blueprint, we worked on ourselves and the necessary precautions we have to place on the people that surround us. Today, we are going to focus on setting an expectation on God. God tells us in the book of Malachi that we can prove Him at His Word. We can set an expectation on Him and not be afraid. This can apply to our family and their protection, the security of our health and the security of our finances. When I tithe and give of my time, I'm not just saying that "I'm committed to You," but "God, you are committed to me." It is a covenant that cannot be broken, regardless of my circumstance. Without you knowing it, His hand covered you even when you didn't want to be covered. His love endures and His promise is sure because His blueprint doesn't have a return policy.

One of God's greatest attributes is that He is a keeper, defender and a protector. It's in His nature to fight for what is His. He's a jealous God and protects His investment, that is why today's scripture says He will not slumber or sleep as He keeps us. Our job in this protection is to stand back and watch Him protect us. If your project is to get your family back together because your children rebelled, you have to set an expectation on God and remind Him of His word. If it's to restore your marriage, do the same and set the expectation. He won't let you down.

Today's Declaration:

Lord, today I declare protection over my life and over my home. Thank you because there is no weapon that is formed against me and my home that can prosper. You love us and have promised to keep us, so we thank you for that. We thank you for assigning angels to our right and left, and for keeping us even when we haven't noticed.

In Jesus name, Amen.

Day 26 – Details

Today's Scripture: Matthew 25:23 (NKJV)

23 His lord said to him, 'Well done, good and faithful servant; you have been faithful over a few things, I will make you ruler over many things. Enter into the joy of your lord.'

Today's Thought:

I heard a preacher say, "Excellence is not being a perfectionist. Excellence is saying that there is something we can always improve on." After every project, you see that someone always goes back to make sure that everything was done according to plan. If something was missed, they go back and try to correct it and make the necessary adjustments. It typical that during the construction phase, something was missed and needs to either be replaced or patched up. But again, if we are going to do this, we are going to do it the right way. I'm not speaking about being a perfectionist, I'm referring to doing things the way that they should be done.

I've learned that it's the details in a ministry or in a project that determine its growth and success. Some people just aren't worried with the small things. This is why the scripture today reminds us that we have to learn how to manage the little we have been entrusted with before we start asking for the world. Before we ask God to help us save the entire city, we have to learn to manage small groups or small congregations. We have to learn to manage our alarm clock and get to work on time before we ask God to give us our own business.

Is it possible that we think that we own something God has just made us a steward of? When you are a steward, that means that whatever is in your hands, you are just maintaining and making sure that it is running correctly. Because God is interested in the details, my job is to make sure I learn how to perfect the little things in my life and manage them correctly before I ask for more. If don't know how to manage a $20,000 a year salary, what makes you think you can manage $40,000 a year? Mathematics and common sense tell us mismanagement is mismanagement on whatever tax bracket you are.

No matter how long it takes, we are going to get down to making sure the details have been taken care of. By the time we finish this project, I'm going to make sure I don't regret anything because it was done the right way to begin with. I'm going to make sure I use my money wisely. I'm also going to make sure that I get to work on time and pay attention to the details, before I ask for God to overwhelm my life with more.

Today's Declaration:

Lord, thank you for the spirit of excellence that is on my life. May I never become complacent with the status-quo, but continually grow in my gift and craft. My desire is to glory and honor to your name in the way I pay attention to the details in my life. Allow to align the things that need to be fixed and order the things that I currently mismanage.

In Jesus name, Amen.

Day 27 – Clean Up

Today's Scripture: Psalm 107:19-21 (NKJV)

19
Then they cried out to the Lord in their trouble,
And He saved them out of their distresses.
20
He sent His word and healed them,
And delivered them from their destructions.
21
Oh, that men would give thanks to the Lord for His goodness,
And for His wonderful works to the children of men!

Today's Thought:

It's clean-up day! This is the day that we pick up all the tools, left over materials and throw out all the trash. We are literally starting with a clean slate. This could mean that for the marriage that you are working on, it's a fresh start and because we got down to the details, we can make sure that we are ready for this new season of our lives before we move any furniture in.

Today, we have to go through the entire house and make sure that we get some glass cleaner and clean the smudges that we left behind because of installation. We have to pull out the broom and mop, and pick up the saw dust that fell in that corner no one noticed. We are cleaning the house before we move a piece of furniture in. We are able to see the things someone else might miss if there were furniture and area rugs there. Because we are detail-oriented, we are going to clean this thing right.

I believe this is the phase where you can speak with your spouse, significant other, family, or friends, make sure that everything is out for everyone to see. Just like David said in today's scripture, His word has the power to heal and deliver. This means that you have to say it all and don't leave anything on your heart or in your head. The important thing is that we are doing this together and everyone is able to be involved in the cleaning and healing process. You can't brush anything under the rug, because there is no rug! When there is something there to cover it up, we typically do so that we don't hurt the other person. But true healing requires exposure and vulnerability. Just like going to a doctor, you can't just tell them that something hurts. They want to know how it happened and where it hurts. This would be the place of transparency.

This is a great place for healing. We've made sure that this thing was built right, and that nothing is going to hold us back from living God's original design for our lives.

Today's Declaration:

Lord, today I thank you for finding me in my despair and for healing all the pain of my past. I thank you for not covering up my mistakes but loving me through them and giving me your grace to overcome the guilt of committing them. I declare healing from my past as I move into the future. Thank you for allowing me to be vulnerable and transparent with the people that I love and the people that care for me. Make me whole.

In Jesus name, Amen.

Day 28 – Move-in Ready

Today's Scripture: Numbers 13:1-2 (NKJV)

13 And the Lord spoke to Moses, saying, 2 "Send men to spy out the land of Canaan, which I am giving to the children of Israel; from each tribe of their fathers you shall send a man, every one a leader among them."

Today's Thought:

Time to move in! The day has arrived when I begin to move in my clothes and the essentials. This is also the day when the new furniture arrives and I'm able to show pride in what I've built. The enemy is typically very frustrated by this point because you were never supposed to get this far. As soon as God gives you a promise on something, that is the moment that the enemy moves in and interferes with what He has declared.

If we see the story of Moses and the twelve spies, we see that when they went to spy out the land God had promised them, there were what appeared to be giants occupying that territory. The enemy is going to send opposition to stop you from living in it and enjoying it. This doesn't always come in the form of people, but he can bring discouragement and anxiety to you about what you are about to walk into. I've found that when you are closest to your greatest breakthrough, you encounter your greatest opposition. That opposition, just like the ten spies that came back with a bad report, comes from yourself own self-doubt and lack of self-esteem. Today, we add a new value to ourselves and the purpose for our lives. You have to place value on it because God took His time in designing you. That makes you of value! Regardless of what thought comes to your mind and what fear try to creep up, learn to trust Him through this transition. Transition is tough, but also necessary in the seasons of life.

Don't expect the worse, but also don't expect for things to go silky smooth. As you know, things don't always work out as you had planned, but they still do work out one way or the other. By this, I am telling you that move-in day requires peace and trust. Today is the day that you occupy the promise and the design. This is the day you begin to walk in the ministry that God has called you to. Just like the word came to Moses, the word comes to you to execute and don't be afraid to move into what already belongs to you as a son of God. Opposition is going to be there, but that is the sign and indication to you that what is before you, is greater than what is behind you.

Today's Declaration:

Lord, today I thank you for driving out all of my enemies out of the land that belongs to me. I declare that I will occupy every promise that you have made for me and my family. I will not die until I see what you've promised come to pass. Today, I walk into your promises with confidence, knowing that every enemy has been defeated and what is before me is so much greater than what is behind me.

In Jesus name, Amen.

Day 29 – Inspect

Today's Scripture: Psalm 139:23-24 (NKJV)

23
Search me, O God, and know my heart;
Try me, and know my anxieties;
24
And see if there is any wicked way in me,
And lead me in the way everlasting.

Today's Thought:

Inspections have to be thorough. When insuring your house or property with an insurance carrier, they will typically require an inspection on the property. This makes sure that the house was built correctly and provides an assessment value to the property to see how much it needs to be insured for.

When speaking to our present state, we have to inspect the final result. We look through it, make sure there are no open doors, make sure we have picked up all the dust and looked everything through again. We have to inspect because inspection will provide a final value to what we've built. The problem is that you cannot inspect the property by yourself. This is where you need the help of an inspector. An inspector has been trained to spot fault, danger and potential loss. This is why many times, before you purchase a house, the lender will require an inspection. They want to make sure that before you commit to that property and use their money to buy it, you are not being taken advantage of by a bad seller that is trying to get rid of a bad house.

David asked God to search him completely and to try him. This is the role of an inspector. Depending on what you are building, inspectors come in the form of pastors, marriage and family counselors, financial advisors and covenant friends. These inspectors come and won't let you get into anything that cannot serve as a benefit to you. Some of our covenant relationships and loved ones know more than what we give them credit for. The key is knowing that you can trust them with that information and let them see it all. On the same taken, be careful who you open up to. Inspectors are there to help, not just expose. Their presence provides a level of accountability that is needed to grow and to move forward.

Today's Declaration:

Lord, thank you that today you are inspecting yourself and sending inspectors to check my heart and my motives. Today, I want you to make sure that what I have built will last and not just pass because it was not inspected correctly. Search me, lead me, and find within me the things that still need to be sharpened and corrected.

In Jesus name, Amen.

Day 30 – Assessment

Today's Scripture: 1 Chronicles 16:34 (NKJV)

Oh, give thanks to the Lord, for He is good!
For His mercy endures forever.

Today's Thought:

Think of what you've built over the last thirty days. This brings a sense of satisfaction and peace. Assessing includes thanksgiving. This is the time and place in your life where you have to look back and asses where you've come from and where you are now. If you were to look at how far you've come, you're able to see something so critical that many people miss. This is called progress. The word progress is scary to many because it means that I'm not where I prefer to be, but I'm not where I was before. Progress is incubated in process. These last thirty days weren't easy. I'm sure there were moments where you wanted to give up and throw in the towel like many others would have, but you didn't. Losing weight isn't easy. I've tried it myself several times and when I've made some type of progress in my weight loss, I look back and assess how far I've come. This is a moment of pride and of self-examination. I would celebrate with a quick celebratory dinner that I wouldn't usually indulge in.

Today's scripture tells us that we have to give thanks to the Lord because He is good. Are all the things you've been working for in perfect order or exactly how you want them to be? I'm sure that they are not. But you still have to be thankful. Thanksgiving will shift your attitude and not let you focus on the things that didn't work out, but draw your attention to the things that He has done. If you don't sit back, give thanks and assess, you cannot learn for the next project.

Today's Declaration:

Lord, today I thank you for what you have done and for what you are doing in my life. Although not everything is perfect, I thank you because you make all things good in their time and season. Give me the right perspective to assess the great things that you have pulled me out of, brought me into and walked me through. Today, my heart is thankful because although the process has not been easy, you've allowed me to build something that I didn't think I could do. And for that alone, I am grateful.

In Jesus name, Amen.

Day 31 – Rest

Today's Scripture: Genesis 2:2 (NKJV)

2 *And on the seventh day God ended His work which He had done, and He rested on the seventh day from all His work which He had done.*

Today's Thought:

Even God, on the seventh day, rested and knew that what He made was good. If God rested, how much more should we learn to rest? Our faith in God is the most important ingredient in life because life itself is void without Him. It's like having spaghetti without the sauce or eating peanut butter without jelly. Something is just always missing and doesn't seem right.

He is the creator of the universe and the giver of every good gift. If you've applied this devotional to your marriage and trying to get it to work again, by now, you should see some progress. If you've applied this to your professional career, by now, you should see some progress. You should now sit back and rest. Rest is not laziness. Rest is confidence in God. That although I can't do it all, I know the God who can work it all and do it the right way the first time. Rest is important, even when we are speaking about the healing of our bodies, the protection of our families, our finances and those things that we hold dear to ourselves.

When we speak about rest, we are not talking about sleep. Sleep is something that you do for about 8 hours as an action. Rest is a constant position that you are in and never moved from. When you're dealing with the issues of life, you need to be in a constant position of rest. God's rest comes with His joy and His peace. This means that while others are going crazy about something, you are not because you are in rest. It doesn't mean that you are desensitized to what is going on around you. You just don't react like they do because you are at rest.

Rest is a gift of the Spirit that has to be asked for on a daily basis. Now that you have finished this devotional, ask for the rest of God to come over your life every day to live out in faith what He has designed for you. Although it might seem like a huge task, He will give you the rest to do it and not be stressed or be anxious.

Today's Declaration:

Lord, today thank you for rest. Thank you for granting me supernatural rest from everything that is overwhelming me and burdening me. The design for my life can seem overwhelming, but I thank you because you are filling me now with your rest and with your peace. This is a rest that the world doesn't understand and won't comprehend. Thank you because rest is coming to all areas of my life. As far as my relationships, family, career and money, you are giving me your rest.

In Jesus name, Amen.

Final Words

Is this the end? Not at all. If you ask any couple what's their secret to keeping the flame alive, they will tell you to never let it go out. That means that although you're done with this phase, you never stop building. If you're a true builder, your mindset is always constantly thinking about the next project as soon as you finish the last one.

There are so many parts to our lives that always need fixing, repair or a complete overhaul. This is where you go through the blueprint again and make sure that you don't miss a single detail. The greatest misconception is that we don't need help, or that everything that needs to be done already is. Another one that people tell themselves is like the old saying; "If it's not broke, don't fix it." If it not working correctly, you should look into fixing it now while it's not such a huge project and hasn't become a large problem. Some find themselves crying when demolition team has arrived, instead of making the needed repairs to the property while it is still standing. While you have the time, take advantage and invest in what really matters and what really has value.

Is it always going to be done the same? Maybe not. This time, you may choose to do it by yourself. The next time, you might want to read this with your loved one(s). It will be completely up to you. 2 Corinthians 1:20 tells us that "God's promises are yes," but they also require our participation. Trust Him, the One who started the good work to finish what He started.